Crafty girl™

beauty

crafty girl™

beauty

things to make and do

by Jennifer Traig
and Julianne Balmain

CHRONICLE BOOKS

SAN FRANCISCO

Library of Congress Cataloging-in-Publication Data available.

ISBN 0-8118-2999-5

Printed in Singapore

Line drawings by Stephanie Sadler
Designed and illustrated by Gayle Steinbeigle

Distributed in Canada by Raincoast Books
9050 Shaughnessy Street
Vancouver, British Columbia V6P 6E5

10 9 8 7 6 5 4 3

Chronicle Books LLC
85 Second Street
San Francisco, California 94105
www.chroniclebooks.com

Crafty Girl™ is a registered trademark of Chronicle Books LLC.

Notice: This book is intended as an educational and informational guide. With any craft project, check product labels to make sure that the materials you use are safe and nontoxic. "Nontoxic" is a description given to any substance that does not give off dangerous fumes or contain harmful ingredients (such as chemicals or poisons) in amounts that could endanger a person's health.

acknowledgments

says Jennifer~

Thanks to my parents for encouraging crafty flights of fancy and to my sister Victoria for copiloting; to Tali Koushmaro, Miriam and Mitzi Schleicher, and the staff and students at Woodland Montessori Children's House for being so generous with ideas and input; to Peter McGrath, Angela Hernandez, and Daniel Archer for putting up with a messy test kitchen; to Mikyla Bruder for being a superlative editor and friend and for giving me a job; and to Stephanie Sadler, Gayle Steinbeigle, Laura Lovett, Jodi Davis and the rest of the Chronicle crew.

says Julianne~

This book is for Judy B. (AKA Mom), who endured and even encouraged the scalding lemon peel facial, my first home-made beauty treatment. Many thanks to the team at Chronicle Books for their inspiration, creativity, and hard work. Further thanks to all the beautiful crafty people who gave us hot tips and shared their secret formulas. May your hair always shine and your skin never feel rough or dry.

table of contents

A side from the pure sport of it, there are three good reasons for a crafty girl to apply her skills and creativity to the realm of beauty and body care: look great, smell great, feel great.

Are you a sleek urbanite? Are you a glamour queen hiding out in suburbia? Is your look tribal chic? Maybe you have a flair for ponytails and jeans. No matter what your style, *Crafty Girl: Beauty* offers inspiration for making you a more dazzling creature, even if that just means having healthier pores and shinier locks. Whipping up your own products to pamper, purify, and enhance your natural aura of health and vigor also saves you money, ensures that the stuff on your skin and hair is natural and nontoxic, and prevents a few of the world's bunnies and other test critters from having to wear your moisturizer and lip gloss before you do. Best of all, your creations will be entirely yours, endowed with whatever scents you choose and tailored to your personal needs (as in, "I have a need to smear avocado all over my face"). An eye-opening journey of discovery in the land of lotions and potions, *Crafty Girl: Beauty* is your ticket to supple skin, radiant cheeks, glitzy nails, cozy toes, and a new sense of empowerment on the fragrance front.

Basic Supplies

The first step is demystification. Face it crafty girls, those froufrou goodies at the cosmetics counters in department stores may contain scientifically engineered hydrolyzed sea kelp extract, but mostly they're made of water, oils, and fragrances. You will be amazed at how far you can get with a few inexpensive, pure, natural ingredients found in supermarkets, drugstores, and natural foods stores. Beauty basics include:

 Oils and moisturizers: mineral oil, sweet almond oil, jojoba oil, castor oil, olive oil, beeswax, cocoa butter, avocado, banana

- ❋ **Exfoliants: oats, sea salt**
- ❋ **Astringents: lemon juice, grapefruit juice, distilled white vinegar**
- ❋ **Soothers, refreshers: cucumber slices, chamomile tea bags, baking soda**

Stock up on an assortment of these basics, and you are on your way to looking gorgeous.

As with many other pivotal moments in your life, the decision to make your own soap will lead you to a nice, big craft store for supplies. If you don't have one nearby, there are tons of places to buy soap-making ingredients on the Web, such as www.sunsoap.com (they sell essential oils too) and www.craftcave.com. Glycerin soap base is widely available, sometimes at the ubiquitous discount chains, and is clear, gentle, and easy to work with. Note: Glycerin Rule #1 is, it looks like water, but it is **not** okay to drink. Don't leave it sitting around in a water glass. You can substitute Neutrogena in a pinch. Don't fear the soap.

The next important step—and perhaps the best part about crafty beauty—is choosing a perfume or essential oil (or several) for adding fragrance to your creations. A tiny vial of essential oil lets you have an aromatherapy experience while you perfume all kinds of soaps, shampoos, moisturizers, scrubs, and baths, because it takes only a drop or two to make any concoction smell heavenly. Essential oils of lemon, orange, peppermint, rose, lavender, vanilla, and cinnamon are all crowd pleasers. For more exotic scents, you might try amber, cedar, eucalyptus, rosemary, ginger, or almond, and when you are ready for a truly deluxe experience you can combine two or three oils for a signature fragrance all your own. Essential oils are available at most natural foods stores, some drugstores, many bath and skin-care shops, and a number of Web sites, including www.bodytime.com. Note: Aromatherapy Rule #1 is, always use glass containers (essential oils react with plastic). Start looking for pretty bottles now.

Ultimately, the crafty girl approach to beauty is as much about relaxation and celebrating your own personal beauty as it is about smearing stuff on your face and gluing sequins to your shoulders. The recipes included here will give you simple, inexpensive, low-commitment ways to pamper and rejuvenate good old you at the end of a long day or a tough week. Even if your life is nothing but Sunday morning cake and sunshine, you'd probably still enjoy a peppermint steam facial now and then. And who would turn down a Nourishing Nectar smoothie for tub-time sipping? (Not us. Jennifer is running a bath right now.) These recipes are just the beginning—they're sure to give you plenty of ideas for new creations. After you blend a new beauty concoction, be sure to craft a worthy container, too. Keep self-adhesive labels on hand to decorate with stamps and glitter. Title your product and write the name in fancy script: "Firming Cider Skin Tonic #12, Manufactured by Hand in the 21st Century, for Producing a Radiant Glow about the Face."

In the great game of life, originality counts. Who else could fashion a full line of glittery lip gloss, body sparkles, and high-glam nail polish, all in precisely the same shade and luminosity as your favorite earrings? Who else could make that see-through soap with the plastic hula dancer inside? Only you, crafty girl. Whether you bottle it up and give it away, or lock yourself in the bathroom for the next decade anointing your limbs with delicious-smelling oils, is up to you. All we ask is that you hose out the tub after an herbal soak, and leave a tea bag or two in the kitchen cupboard in case somebody actually wants to make tea (weird).

From exotic nail decorations to scruffy, sea salt exfoliants and refreshing citrus toner, the recipes in this book will inspire you to make over your life for a brand-new you. Or maybe the same old you, but with smoother skin and mendhi henna-esque watercolor designs decorating your ankles. The thing is to get started right away. There is probably a vial of vanilla extract in the kitchen. If you can pop out to a supermarket and pick up some coarse sea salt (which should run you about a dollar) and a bottle of baby oil, you will have what it takes to rid your hide of dry, dead, natural-glow-inhibiting skin cells. What are you waiting for mama? The day is here and the night is young. It's time to look your best.

The Danger Zone

Important note: Even though your concoctions will be made of simple, natural components (glitter excepted), there is always the possibility that your skin will say "no way" to an ingredient. Some crafty girls, for example, are allergic to the seemingly friendly avocado. Since you may not know what you are sensitive to until it's too late, always, always, always test your brew on a small patch of skin, such as the inside of your forearm, and wait about 20 minutes before you slather it all over your body. If it makes your skin look red or irritated or feel itchy, hot, or otherwise unpleasant, skip it.

Some recipes in this book require you to boil water, heat oils, pour hot liquids, and use a knife. These are risky maneuvers which require caution, patience, proper equipment, and, to be extra safe, an adult's help. Grab an adult any time you plan to use the stove, microwave, or a sharp knife.

Don't eat anything that isn't obviously food. While all the recipes in the book call for natural ingredients, only the food recipes are edible.

part **1**

face

apple-a-day
toner

Toners are like exercise for your skin—they keep your pores lean and mean. For an apple-cheeked fresh face, try this beauty brew. It's especially gentle, so it's okay for dry skin.

You will need:

²/₃ cup apple cider vinegar

²/₃ cup water

10-ounce decorative bottle with a narrow opening, washed and dried (an apple-shaped Martinelli's Gold Medal juice bottle works great)

Homemade label (optional)

1 foot red satin ribbon (optional)

Cotton balls

[1] In a small bowl, stir together vinegar and water. Pour the mixture into your decorative bottle.

[2] If you like, attach your label to the bottle and tie the ribbon around the neck. Instant cosmetic boutique chic, yes?

[3] Shake well and apply toner to your freshly washed face with a cotton ball. Don't wash it off, just let it dry. Admire your tiny pores. Follow with your usual moisturizer, if you use one.

Makes 10 ounces.

 Note An old jam or jelly jar makes a neat container for cotton balls.

tingly
toner

This bracing brew is as refreshing as a cold glass of lemonade on a hot summer day. It's astringent, so it's particularly good for oily skin.

You will need:

1 cup witch hazel (in the soap section at the supermarket)

8-ounce decorative bottle with a narrow opening, washed and dried (an empty glass lemon-juice bottle makes a nice touch, but any bottle will do)

15 drops lemon essential oil

Homemade label (optional)

1 foot yellow satin ribbon (optional)

Cotton balls

[1] Pour witch hazel into your decorative bottle. Add essential oil. Cap bottle securely and shake well.

[2] Attach your label and tie the ribbon around the neck for a polished presentation, if you like.

[3] Shake well and swipe toner over your freshly washed face with a cotton ball. Allow to dry while enjoying the delicious lemony fragrance. Feels like sunshine and a cool breeze in a bottle.

Makes 8 ounces.

desert rose

moisturizer

Do your cheeks feel more like the Sahara dunes than dewy petals? Try this easy moisturizer. It's light and oil free, so it's great for oily skin, too.

You will need:

1 cup water

½ cup fresh rose petals (red ones are best, since they turn the brew a lovely pink; consult the gardener before you whack his or her prized American Beauties)

16-ounce bottle with cap, any shape, washed and dried

1 cup liquid glycerin (available at drugstores)

1 tablespoon aloe vera juice (available at health food stores)

Homemade label (optional)

3 small dried red roses with stems (optional)

1 foot red or pink satin ribbon (optional)

[1] In a small saucepan, heat water and rose petals just until boiling. Let the rose water cool, then strain out petals.

[2] Pour rose water into your decorative bottle. Pour in glycerin and aloe vera juice. Cap bottle securely and shake well to blend.

[3] If you like, attach your label, and tie dried roses around the bottle with the satin ribbon.

[4] Store your moisturizer in the refrigerator. It doesn't have any preservatives, so it can go bad within a couple of weeks if you leave it out (if it's refrigerated it should be fine for a month or two; if it starts looking murky or smelling a bit off, toss it). Plus, it will feel nice and cool when you apply it. Shake gently before each use. Smooth some on, avoiding the eye area, whenever your skin feels parched or rough.

Makes about 16 ounces.

instant milk-and-honey
mask

Milk and honey make baked goods firm, soft, and shiny. They do the same for your skin. Indulge in this rich treatment when your face is feeling dull and dry.

You will need:

1 egg white (see note, page 27)

1 tablespoon honey

3 tablespoons powdered milk

1 teaspoon liquid glycerin (glycerin is easy to find at most drugstores, but you could also substitute a few drops of vitamin E oil—if you can't find liquid vitamin E, break open a couple of vitamin E capsules)

Note We know we've said it before, but just to be sure, we'll say it again. Glycerin looks like water, but is not to be ingested. Don't leave it around in an unlabeled container, and be sure to wash your mixing bowl and utensils thoroughly after use.

[1] In a small bowl, stir together egg white, honey, powdered milk, and glycerin until blended.

[2] Apply to face, avoiding your eye area. (Go ahead and use it all, because it won't keep.)

[3] Sit back and relax for 15 minutes. If your favorite soothing CD is spinning, that's three blissful songs.

[4] Rinse off with warm water.

Makes one mask.

greek goddess
mask

In Greece, lemon and eggs make a delicious soup called avgolemono. They also make a great facial mask for oily skin. Smooth some on and 15 minutes later you'll feel like Aphrodite.

You will need:

1 egg white (see note)

Juice of $\frac{1}{2}$ lemon, strained

[1] In a small bowl, lightly beat together egg white and lemon juice until blended.

[2] Apply to face, avoiding the eye area. Leave on for 15 minutes.

[3] Rinse off with warm water and follow with a good moisturizer.

Makes one mask.

To separate the egg white from the yolk, carefully crack and open the shell over a small bowl, keeping the contents inside one of the shell halves (make sure the yolk stays intact). Transfer the yolk back and forth between the two halves of the shell, letting the egg white drip into the bowl until only the yolk remains in the shell. Discard the yolk and shell, or see page 81 for a good yolk use.

emerald
emollient

> It's easy to make moisturizers at home. You should be able to find most of these ingredients at any drugstore, and craft stores will carry the rest. You'll end up with a rich, soothing cream as green as an emerald—just the thing for dry skin.

You will need:

1 cup green aloe vera juice

1 teaspoon vitamin E oil (if you can't find the liquid, break open a few vitamin E capsules)

5 to 10 drops essential oil or perfume oil in your favorite scent

$3/4$ ounce grated cosmetic-grade beeswax (try a craft store if your drugstore doesn't carry any)

$1/2$ cup vegetable oil

Double boiler (a pan with another pan inside it that allows you to cook in the upper pan by boiling water in the lower)

Electric hand mixer

13-ounce decorative jar, washed and dried

Homemade label

1 foot green satin ribbon

Note For a fanciful package on the cheap, wash out any old jar—jam and jelly jars often have a nice shape. Grab some acrylic craft paint, craft glue, and a handful of flat-back emerald gems and green rhinestones. Paint the lid white, silver, green, or any other color. Let it dry and then glue a few choice emeralds in place. Add your label and ribbon for that haute cosmetic chic.

[1] In a mixing bowl, stir together aloe vera juice, vitamin E oil, and essential oil until combined. Set aside.

[2] In the top of a double boiler set over simmering water, melt beeswax with vegetable oil, stirring until smooth.

continued on next page

[3] Pour a slow, steady stream of the melted wax mixture into the aloe vera mixture while blending with an electric mixer set on the slowest setting. When the mixture is smooth and thoroughly blended, pour it into the decorative jar.

[4] Attach your label in place and tie the satin ribbon around the jar.

[5] Store your moisturizer in the refrigerator. (It doesn't have any preservatives, so it can spoil. Stored in the fridge, it should be fine for six weeks or so.) Apply to skin daily or whenever it feels dry (always avoid the eye area).

Makes about 13 ounces.

three square meals for

your face

> *Your skin gets hungry, too. Give it the nutrition it needs with this all-day meal plan.*

Breakfast

This gentle, exfoliating porridge is just right for taking off dead skin cells.

You will need:

2 tablespoons rolled oats

2 tablespoons plain yogurt

2 teaspoons honey

 In a small bowl, combine all ingredients and stir until blended.

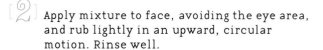 Apply mixture to face, avoiding the eye area, and rub lightly in an upward, circular motion. Rinse well.

Makes enough for one application.

continued on next page

Lunch

Soothe and smooth your skin with ingredients from the salad bar.

You will need:

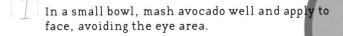

$\frac{1}{2}$ ripe avocado, peeled

2 slices cucumber

[1] In a small bowl, mash avocado well and apply to face, avoiding the eye area.

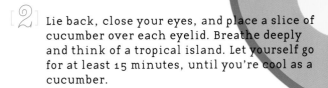

[2] Lie back, close your eyes, and place a slice of cucumber over each eyelid. Breathe deeply and think of a tropical island. Let yourself go for at least 15 minutes, until you're cool as a cucumber.

[3] Rinse and go back to your day feeling refreshed.

Makes enough for one application.

Note

Some people are sensitive to the acids in fruits and vegetables, especially avocado. If either the avocado or the cucumber makes your skin itch, sting, or tingle, you're one of them. Remove the offending fruit or vegetable immediately and wash skin well. If it makes you feel bad, it won't make you look good.

Dinner

This nighttime steam treatment gets out the day's grime and tension. It's like a relaxing cup of tea for your face. Get an adult to help with the boiling and pouring of the water, and don't get your face too close to the hot steam.

You will need:

2 cups water

2 herbal tea bags (use peppermint for oily skin, chamomile for dry skin)

Towel

[1] In a saucepan, bring water to a boil and add tea bags. Reduce heat and simmer for five minutes. Remove pan from stove.

33

[2] Very carefully pour the contents of the pan into a large, heatproof bowl. Test the steam by putting your hand at least 12 inches above the bowl. If it's okay, put your face at least 12 inches above the pan and drape a towel over your head to create a steam tent. Stay in your steam tent until you feel good and relaxed and your skin feels dewy.

[3] Rinse your face with cool water and pat dry.

Makes one steam treatment.

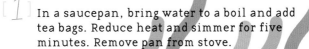

zit repair kit

Zits happen. If they happen more often than you'd like, take heart; it means your skin is producing the oils that will prevent wrinkles later on. In the meantime, use your crafty superpowers to camouflage unwanted arrivals. Here are some quick-fix tips.

You may need any or all of the following:

Toothpaste (the white kind, not gel)

Eyedrops (like Visine)

Eyebrow pencil

Tiny adhesive bandage (optional)

A really good attitude

Dab a little toothpaste on the zit and leave it there for several hours—overnight is best. This sounds crazy but it does indeed work. Gently wash toothpaste off and pat dry. Your zit should be zapped and on its way out.

If you don't have time for the toothpaste treatment, apply some eyedrops to the offending area. The drops should get the red out, just like they do to your peepers.

 If the zit is small and not too red, draw a mole on it with an eyebrow pencil. Voilà! Instead of a pimple, you now have a glamorous beauty mark. (Warning: High-risk behavior. If you are among friends who happen to know you are not Cindy Crawford and that is not a beauty mark, you will be hosed. Best for emergencies among strangers only.)

 If all else fails, cover the zit with a tiny bandage. Tell everyone you scratched your face doing something heroic, such as getting a cat down out of a tree. (Warning: No one will believe this. In fact, if you actually happen to scratch your face and you put a bandage there, everyone will assume you have a horrible zit. Life is so unfair.)

 You could just leave it alone and try to forget about it. Why should something so small ruin your moment?

 Regarding the Big Squeeze: It's really best to avoid it, but if you must squeeze, take a hot shower first to open your pores and soften the skin. If one light squeeze doesn't do the trick, let it ride or risk making things much worse.

shine on

Lip-smacking glitter gloss is easy to make. This one smells as good as it looks. Don't touch the melted beeswax, it's hot.

You will need:

2 teaspoons grated cosmetic-grade beeswax

2 tablespoons plus one teaspoon sweet almond, jojoba, or castor oil

1 teaspoon honey

3 to 5 drops essential oil (lemon, orange, or peppermint)

Fine glitter (available at craft and art supply stores; make sure it's nontoxic)

Small jars, washed and dried (if you're using store-bought lip balm jars, you'll need about five)

[1] In a small saucepan, melt beeswax with oil over very low heat, stirring until smooth. When the beeswax is melted, remove from heat. Add honey and stir until blended.

[2] After the mixture has cooled a bit, add essential oil and stir until blended. When it's completely cool, stir in your glitter and transfer to little jars.

Makes about 1½ ounces.

Instant Gratification Variation

Measure out 2 tablespoons petroleum jelly and add a few drops of citrus or mint essential oil and a sprinkle of fine glitter. Stir until blended and you're on your way.

lemon

orange

peppermint

gypsy gems

For that special event when nothing but the best will do, add the glimmer of precious gems to your natural glow. Your skin's the perfect setting for these glue-on rhinestones and jewels.

You will need:

Eyelash glue (available at most drugstores)

Flat-back rhinestones, beads, or pearls (available at craft stores)

[1] Test eyelash glue by brushing some on the inside of your wrist. Wait 15 minutes. If no itching or redness occurs, proceed to step 2. If itching or redness does occur, wash your wrist with soap and water and go *au natural*.

[2] Brush eyelash glue on the back of your gem.

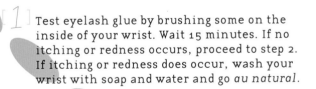

[3] Apply to skin. Try a design on your forehead or cheekbones, glue a rhinestone mole to your cheek, dot tiny rhinestones around your eyes or along your collarbone, make a faux pearl necklace, add glittering blue teardrops to your ankle, or give one shoulder a fancy curlicue.

[4] Go out on the town and sparkle like a star. Use eye-makeup remover to take off your gems.

part 2

bath and body

critter-in-the-middle
soap treats

Like prehistoric ants trapped in amber, plastic bugs or figurines float magically inside these bars of translucent soap. Feature your favorite creatures or try plastic hearts, stars, aliens, nuns, hula dancers, babies, dinosaurs, or any other tiny treasures that will stand up to heat, soap, and water.

You will need:

16 ounces glycerin soap base (look for it at craft stores, along with other soap-making supplies—if you can't find any, just use a transparent soap like Neutrogena)

5 to 10 drops perfume or essential oil, such as lavender, vanilla, or eucalyptus, for adding a delicious fragrance (optional)

Soap molds (buy them at a craft store or improvise with available kitchen supplies; ice cube trays work well, and you can also use glasses, Pyrex cups, or ceramic ramekins—almost anything will work, as long as it's not aluminum, which reacts with the lye in soaps)

Petroleum jelly or vegetable shortening

Small plastic creatures or whatever you plan to trap in your soap

Wax paper

[1] Get an adult to help you chop up the soap into small chunks.

[2] In a medium-size, microwave-safe mixing bowl, melt the soap base in microwave on high in 1-minute intervals.

[3] Add perfume oil, if using.

[4] Grease soap molds with petroleum jelly or vegetable shortening. Carefully pour the melted soap base into the molds until they are filled halfway. Allow to cool for five or ten minutes, then place plastic creatures on top. Pour the rest of the soap base over the creatures, until the molds are full.

43

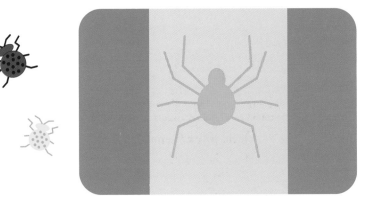

continued on next page

[4] Cool thoroughly, then release from molds. Soap shrinks as it cools, so you shouldn't have any problem getting your soaps loose, but if you do, carefully jimmy them free with a butter knife. Wrap with wax paper and store in a cool, dry place.

Makes about 4 bars, depending on size of molds.

Flower Power Soap Variation

Instead of a plastic critter, float a silk or plastic flower inside your soap. Add a floral essential oil to make it smell as pretty as it looks. You can also add soap colorant (available at craft stores) to tint your soap a blossoming shade of pink, purple, or yellow.

citrus

slices

In love with lime? Having tangerine dreams? These tiny citrus soaps are a slice of heaven. Head to a craft store and soon your soap dish will be bursting with fruity orange and lemon flavors. Mix up two or three colors for a citrus-style statement.

You will need:

16 ounces glycerin soap base (look for it at craft stores, along with other soap-making supplies)

5 to 10 drops orange, lemon, lime, grapefruit, or other citrus-scented essential oil or soap scent

1 package soap colorant (orange, yellow, or green; available at craft stores)

Round soap molds, 3 to 4 inches in diameter and at least 1 inch deep (you could also use ramekins or any cylindrical containers, as long as they're not made of aluminum)

Petroleum jelly or vegetable shortening

Toothpick

Wax paper

continued on next page

[1] In a medium-size, microwave-safe mixing bowl, melt soap base in microwave on high in 1-minute intervals.

[2] Add essential oil. Add soap colorant according to directions on package.

[3] Grease soap molds with petroleum jelly or vegetable shortening. Carefully pour soap mixture into molds. When soap is solid but still a little warm to the touch (15 minutes if you're using shallow molds; longer if you're using deeper ones) release from molds. You may need to jimmy them out with a warm butter knife.

[4] Get an adult to help you slice into 1/4-inch-thick rounds (like fat cucumber slices) with a sharp knife (not serrated), then slice the rounds in half, so the soaps resemble fruit slices.

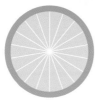

[5] Using a toothpick, trace the outline of rinds and sections onto the soap slices.

[6] Place slices on wax paper and allow to cool completely. Store in a cool, dry place.

Makes about 32 slices, depending on size of molds.

bath
biscuits

Biscuits for the bathtub? Why yes, my skeptical little friend. Toss a couple of these fragrant cookies into a hot bath and let the good times roll. They fizz, they make the water soft and sweet, they smell great, and they come in fun shapes and colors.

You will need:

2 cups fine sea salt

½ cup cornstarch, plus a little extra for rolling out dough

½ cup baking soda

2 eggs

2 tablespoons vegetable oil

1 teaspoon vitamin E oil (if you can't find the liquid, break open some capsules)

5 to 10 drops essential oil or perfume oil in your favorite scent

1 tablespoon dried, chopped lavender, rosemary, or sage (optional)

Food dye (optional)

Rolling pin

Cookie cutters (or use a sturdy glass tumbler to cut rounds)

[1] In a large mixing bowl, stir together sea salt, cornstarch, baking soda, eggs, oil, vitamin E oil, essential oil, and herbs, if using, until the mixture forms a dough. If you want to make biscuits in various colors, separate the dough into three or four balls, add a few drops of food dye to each, and knead until blended.

[2] Dust rolling pin and cutting board or table with extra cornstarch and roll out dough 3/4-inch thick. Cut into fun shapes with cookie cutters, use the opening of a glass to make rounds, or roll dough into little life preservers.

[3] Place 1 inch apart on an ungreased cookie sheet. Bake at 350 degrees for 10 to 12 minutes. Allow to cool.

[4] Store biscuits in a cool, dry place. To use, run a bath, toss a biscuit or two into the water, and enjoy.

Makes about 16 biscuits.

a bit of the
bubbly

A decadent pleasure ever since someone—Cleopatra?—noticed how fun it is to sink into a heap of foamy, glistening suds, the bubble bath is a fine way to end the day. This recipe is so fast it's practically instant. And yet, when the instant is over, you will have your own bottle of custom-scented bubble bath. Mix it up, sink in, wiggle your toes, and let the relaxation begin.

You will need:

10 ounces liquid body wash (a mild, moisturizing shampoo will also work; look for one that's unscented)

1 teaspoon vitamin E oil (or break open some vitamin E capsules)

5 to 10 drops of your favorite essential oil, such as lavender or rose

10-ounce stoppered decorative bottle or empty champagne or sparkling cider bottle (the small "split" size works best) with cork or cap, washed and dried

Length of ribbon and homemade label (optional)

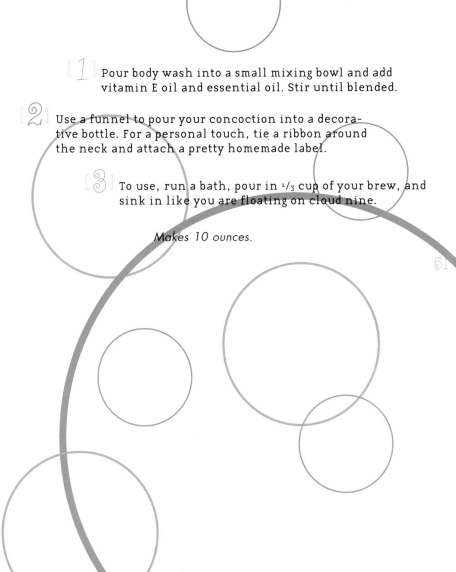

[1] Pour body wash into a small mixing bowl and add vitamin E oil and essential oil. Stir until blended.

[2] Use a funnel to pour your concoction into a decorative bottle. For a personal touch, tie a ribbon around the neck and attach a pretty homemade label.

[3] To use, run a bath, pour in ¹/₃ cup of your brew, and sink in like you are floating on cloud nine.

Makes 10 ounces.

51

milk bath

Milk doesn't just taste smooth and creamy, it also makes your skin feel udderly divine. On those days when it isn't practical to slip into a whole tub of milk—who has the time?—try this creamy brew. You'll emerge as supple as a newborn calf.

You will need:

2 cups powdered milk

1 cup cornstarch

5 to 10 drops essential oil or perfume oil in your favorite scent (we recommend rose, vanilla, or coconut)

32-ounce jar with secure lid

Homemade label and length of ribbon (optional)

[1] Place powdered milk, cornstarch, and essential oil in the jar. Tightly close the lid and shake until well blended. If any oil-powder clumps remain, break them up with your fingers.

[2] If you like, attach a label and tie a ribbon around the bottle.

[3] To use, toss 1/2 cup of your mixture into the bath water and climb right in. It does a body good.

Makes 3 cups.

vanilla
body scrub

Polish that perfect body with a pearly salt scrub in a scrumptious flavor. A pure, natural exfoliant with a built-in moisturizer, it's got it all. And once you have the ingredients on hand, it takes only a second to whip up a batch whenever you feel the need for shiny, glowing skin from head to toe.

You will need:

1/4 cup coarse sea salt

1/4 cup baby oil

1/2 teaspoon vanilla extract (or a couple drops of your favorite perfume oil)

[1] In a small bowl, stir together all ingredients until salt is completely coated with oil.

[2] Take your scrub into the shower with you. When your skin is thoroughly moist, turn off the water and apply with a soft brush or washcloth. Gently massage skin, then rinse off.

Makes enough for one application.

make a splash

Did that long, hot bath zonk you out? Revive yourself with this invigorating after-bath splash. You'll smell great, too.

You will need:

1½ cups water

¼ cup aloe vera juice
(available at health food stores)

¼ cup witch hazel

5 to 10 drops essential oil or perfume oil in your favorite scent (citrus scents work well)

16-ounce decorative bottle, washed and dried

Homemade label (optional)

1 foot satin ribbon (optional)

[1] Pour water, aloe vera juice, witch hazel, and essential oil into your bottle. Cap securely and shake well to blend.

[2] If you like, stick on a label and tie a ribbon around the neck of the bottle.

[3] To use, splash a little all over after your bath and let dry. Feel invigorated.

Makes 16 ounces.

sippers

Treat your body, inside and out, with these delicious smoothies to imbibe while you bathe. Add candlelight, a good book, and a little relaxing music and you have the recipe for bliss any day of the week. Here are two luscious options sure to give your good health a boost.

Nourishing Nectar

You will need:

½ cup plain yogurt

½ banana

½ cup apple juice

2 tablespoons honey

1 tablespoon peanut butter

1 scoop protein powder (optional)

[1] Place all ingredients in a blender and process until completely smooth.

[2] Serve in your favorite frosted glass with a straw.

Makes about 14 ounces.

Fruity Beauty Brew

You will need:

$\frac{1}{2}$ cup plain yogurt

1 cup fresh or frozen fruit chunks
(try berries, bananas, peaches, or
orange segments)

$\frac{1}{3}$ cup juice (try orange, apple,
pineapple, or whatever you like)

$\frac{1}{2}$ cup ice

[1] Place all ingredients in a blender and process
until completely smooth.

[2] Serve in your favorite frosted glass with a straw.

Makes about 16 ounces.

Note Keep a glass in the freezer so you can make
a frosty treat anytime.

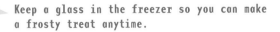

misty spritzers

> You've masked, you've manicured, you've made yourself over. Poor thing, you must be exhausted. Revive yourself with these refreshing concoctions.

Mint Tulip

You will need:

¾ cup mint tea, cooled

¾ cup lemon-lime soda

Ice cubes

Tall frosted glass

Superfine sugar to taste (optional)

2 sprigs fresh mint

[1] Pour tea and soda over ice into your frosted glass. If you want to sweeten your mint tulip, stir in some superfine sugar.

[2] Garnish with fresh mint. Retreat to the front porch and enjoy your mint tulip like a proper Southern belle.

Makes 12 ounces (excluding ice).

Peach Passion

You will need:

$1/3$ cup peach nectar (or substitute a fruit juice you like better; orange is yummy, too)

$1/3$ cup pineapple juice

$2/3$ cup lemon-lime soda

Fancy frosted glass

Orange slice, with a slit cut in it halfway, for fitting on the glass rim

Maraschino cherry

Drink parasol (optional)

[1] Pour peach nectar, pineapple juice, and soda into your frosted glass. Stir to combine.

[2] Garnish with orange slice, cherry, or drink parasol.

[3] Stretch out on a beach chair and enjoy your spritzer while admirers fan you with palm fronds.

Makes about 11 ounces.

herbal
body wrap

You're craving a spa-style indulgence. Mom will freak out if you fill the bathtub with herb-infused mud. Try this recipe for a deeply relaxing herbal wrap instead.

You will need:

6 cups water

3 chamomile tea bags

2 peppermint tea bags

2 sprigs sage or rosemary (optional)

4 to 8 old hand towels (the tea will stain them, so don't use Mom's best)

Clothespins (optional)

Bath towel

[1] Bring water to a boil in a large pot. Remove from heat and add tea bags and herb sprigs, if using. Cover pot and allow to steep for 15 minutes.

[2] Test the temperature of your brew. If it's nice and warm but not hot enough to burn you, it's ready. Remove the tea bags and herb sprigs, using a slotted spoon to scoop them out.

[3] Put the hand towels into the brew. When they're good and wet, remove them and wring them out.

[4] Mummify yourself: Wrap the hand towels around your legs and upper arms. If they won't stay in place, fasten them together with clothespins. Don't wrap your face, neck, feet, or lower arms. If you like, you can drape a hand towel across your torso.

[5] Lay a large bath towel on top of your bed or sofa, lie down, and bliss out for 10 or 15 minutes (and no more). Remove the towels, then let your body cool down for another 15 minutes before jumping in the shower.

Makes one body wrap.

Note   Heat treatments like wraps aren't good for folks with high blood pressure or heart problems. If that's you, skip this one.

cocoa cream

Cocoa butter makes a rich and creamy foundation for this indulgent body moisturizer. Rub it into your shoulders, knees, and elbows for supple smoothness even in the rough spots. The best part: you'll smell like a chocolate bar. Delicious.

You will need:

$\frac{1}{2}$ cup solid vegetable shortening

1 ounce cocoa butter, microwaved until melted (available at drugstores)

6-ounce decorative jar, washed and dried

Homemade label (optional)

[1] Use electric hand mixer to beat shortening and cocoa butter in a bowl until fluffy and blended.

[2] Spoon mixture into the jar, and, if you like, stick your own label on the jar.

[3] Store your Cocoa Cream in the refrigerator. (It doesn't have any preservatives, so it can spoil or separate if left out. Refrigerated, it will stay good for at least six weeks.)

Makes 5 ounces.

glitter glow

Mix your own body glitter in a flash using any glitter you choose. Special evening? Opt for shiny moons and stars. Want to dazzle the beach crowd? Turn your shoulders a glimmering gold. Feeling exotic? Blue-, green-, or rose-colored glitter adds a magical glow to cheeks and temples.

You will need:

63

2 tablespoons hair gel or body lotion

Fine glitter (available at craft and art supply stores)

Tiny jars, washed and dried (if you're using store-bought lip balm jars, you'll need three or four)

[1] Place gel or lotion in a small bowl. Add glitter and mix until you're satisfied with the sparkle intensity.

[2] Transfer your mixture to tiny jars.

[3] Use your fingers to apply a thin layer of your glitter potion wherever you need to shine.

Makes about 1 ounce.

indian

body art

Are mendhi henna tattoos too much for you? Ordinary watercolor paints give you a mendhi look without the time commitment, and they come in a rainbow of pretty colors.

You will need:

Nontoxic, washable watercolor paints (check the label)

Fine paintbrush

[1] Start with clean, dry skin without any moisturizer. Wet your brush and begin painting. Try a delicate dot design on your face, a teardrop on your forehead, elaborate curlicues on your wrists, or hearts and vines or a flower or two on your ankles. Let your artwork dry. Be sure the paint won't be in contact with your clothes, because it can rub off. Stay out of the rain and the swimming pool, too, or you'll be back to the undecorated you in a splash.

[2] When it's time to clean up, your artwork will wash off with soap and water. Lotion or cold cream will remove any lingering color.

part **3**

hands and feet

butterfingers
hand treatment

Bust out the baking supplies, cupcake. Sugar and shortening will soften your skin like nobody's business. Who knew?

You will need:

2 teaspoons granulated sugar

1 tablespoon solid vegetable shortening

2 small plastic bags

Bowl of warm water (big enough to soak both hands in) or heating pad (optional)

Hand lotion

Vanilla extract (optional)

[1] Over the sink, pour sugar into one palm, then rub it all over your hands for 30 seconds or so. The sugar exfoliates dead, rough skin. Rinse your hands and pat dry.

[2] Coat hands liberally with the vegetable shortening. We know, you feel like you just rubbed fried chicken all over them, but you'll thank us later. Tuck hands into the plastic bags so you don't get everything greasy. If you like, you can rest your bagged hands in a bowl of warm (not hot) water or under a warm (not hot) heating pad. Leave shortening on for 10 minutes or so.

[3] Rinse off shortening and pat dry. Smooth on some hand lotion. Then, dab a little vanilla extract on the inside of each wrist. You'll smell as soft and sweet as you feel.

Makes one treatment.

strawberry

tootsie scrub

This easy exfoliant gives new meaning to the phrase "toe jam," and it feels fantastic. The fruit acids soften calluses and rough skin, leaving your feet feeling soft, supple, and ready for warm socks, strappy sandals, or the next step in a full-treatment pedicure.

You will need:

2 tablespoons oil (olive oil is best)

2 teaspoons coarse salt

8 fresh strawberries

Foot brush (optional; some body-care shops carry these)

Hand and body lotion

[1] In a medium-size mixing bowl, stir together oil and salt. Add strawberries. Mash everything together with a fork until the mixture is blended but still somewhat chunky.

[2] Rub the strawberry mixture onto your feet with a foot brush or your hands. Work it around in circles on your heels and other high-impact zones.

[3] Jump in the shower and rinse the mixture off. Rub in some lotion and put socks on those puppies to keep the healing moisture in.

Makes one treatment.

peppermint
toe tingler

You will need:

³⁄₄ cup moisturizing cream (either make your own, using the Emerald Emollient recipe on p. 28 or the Cocoa Cream recipe on p. 62 , or use a store-bought hand and body lotion; petroleum jelly mixed with a squirt or two of hand lotion makes for an extra-rich treat)

12 drops peppermint essential oil

6-ounce decorative jar, washed and dried (an old jam or jelly jar works well)

Homemade label (optional)

Acrylic craft paints and a small paintbrush (optional)

[1] Place moisturizing cream in a small mixing bowl and add peppermint oil. Stir until thoroughly blended.

[2] Spoon mixture into jar. Affix label, if using.

[3] If the lid of the jar is not plain, paint it white and let dry. Paint a sprig of mint in green and any other decorations you like.

[4] To use, slather the cream on your feet, giving them a good rub all around and in between your toes. Prop up your feet, lie back, and enjoy the minty tingle. Store your cream in the refrigerator to keep it nice and cool, and bacteria-free. It should keep for six weeks or so.

Makes about 6 ounces.

personal

Polish

Color chemistry is easy. With some white nail polish as a base and eye shadow in any color, you can make custom-colored nail polish to match all your favorite outfits. Unless, of course, your favorite outfit is plaid.

You will need:

Eye shadow in your color of choice

Paper envelope

Bottle of white nail polish

[1] Crumble some or all of the eye shadow into the envelope. Crush it into a fine powder.

[2] Snip a corner off the envelope to make a tiny funnel. Open the nail polish bottle and slowly add the eye shadow powder to the polish, stirring with the applicator brush until you reach the desired color. You may need to cap the bottle and shake, shake, shake to get everything blended together.

[3] Paint those paws and let dry.

Makes one bottle of polish.

Note

If you want only a little polish, you can whip up a mini-batch in a waxed paper cup, but you'll have to work fast, because it dries quickly. Prepare your eye shadow powder (see step 1) and have your nails clean and ready to paint *before* you pour the white polish into the cup.

lemon soft	shimmer pink	suave mauve
orchid	vamp	sunshine
ice	sky	grass

mondo manicure

An elegant French manicure is lovely for those restrained, highbrow affairs, but when it's time to let loose, good taste is nothing but a roadblock on the highway to big fun. Let your inhibitions go and indulge in a fingernail circus of wild colors, outrageous designs, jewels, gems, and anything else you can find. If you can't get away with flaming fingertips, do your toes. Only you will know the exciting haps going down inside your shoes.

You will need any or all of the following:

Nail polish (several colors for good measure)

World's smallest paintbrush (look for one at a craft store)

Nail polish remover

Nail decals or tiny stickers (flowers, butterflies, or whatever you can find)

Tiny flat-back rhinestones, pearls, or beads (from a craft store)

Eyelash glue (available at most drugstores)

Clear topcoat

[1] First, get some color on those nails. Paint them any shade you like, alternate two colors, or paint every fingernail a different hue. Add more coats as necessary. Be sure to let the enamel dry completely between coats so it doesn't get gummy.

[2] Use a contrasting color and the world's smallest paintbrush to paint on dots, stripes, zigzags, wee flowers, smiley faces, flames, stars, moons, hearts, or even a message spelled out one letter at a time. "Hello" on one hand and "See ya" on the other fits nicely. Clean brush with nail polish remover.

[3] Not feeling all that confident about your painting skills? Use nail decals instead.

[4] Add flat-back rhinestones, pearls, or beads wherever you see fit, using eyelash glue to stick them in place. Allow glue to set thoroughly.

[5] When you've got everything the way you want it and your nails look like something out of Captain Kidd's pirate treasure chest, seal them with a layer or two of clear topcoat and let dry. It's Mondo Manicure show time!

part 4

terrific tresses

squeaky-clean

clarifying potion

If gunky product buildup is weighing down your 'do, try this deep cleansing treatment to get back to nature.

You will need:

2 teaspoons baking soda

12-ounce bottle of shampoo

1/2 cup lemon juice or distilled white vinegar (optional)

[1] Add baking soda to shampoo in bottle and stir with a long spoon or skewer. Distribute a dollop of shampoo through hair, suds up, and rinse well. Condition as usual.

[2] For extra shine, finish with a rinse of lemon juice or vinegar (it gets out that excess conditioner). Be careful not to get either of them in your eyes (ouch). Rinse well with plenty of water. Squeak, squeak—that's clean!

Makes 12 ounces.

deeply decadent
conditioner

Seal in the strength of your locks with this nourishing do-it-yourself indulgence. Rich with moisture and protein, your hair will shine like the glossy mane of a prize-winning show horse . . . or whatever. It will be thoroughly conditioned and shiny—isn't that enough?

You will need:

1 tablespoon oil (olive oil or any vegetable oil is okay)

1 egg yolk (see note, page 82)

Heat cap (a plastic shower cap works)

[1] Put oil in a small dish and microwave for five seconds. You want it warm, but not hot enough to cook the egg.

[2] Add egg yolk to oil and whisk until blended. Work the mixture into your hair.

continued on next page

3   Put on your cap. Leave conditioner in for
    20 minutes or so, then shampoo. Your hair
    is now fabulously luxurious, thanks to the
    bounty of old Mama Nature. While you're
    waiting, use the leftover egg white to make
    the Instant Milk-and-Honey Mask on page 24.

Makes one treatment.

Note   To separate the yolk from the egg white, carefully
       crack and open the shell over a small bowl, keeping
       the contents inside one of the shell halves (make
       sure the yolk stays intact). Transfer the yolk back
       and forth between the two halves of the shell, let-
       ting the egg white drip into the bowl.

color-enhancing
herbal rinses

Honey, you may be too young to dye, but it's never too soon to add a little punch to your natural color, whatever it may be. Try these easy herbal rinses instead of no-return bleaches and harsh color treatments. They'll bring out your highlights subtly and leave your hair even healthier than before.

If you have light hair, you will need:

2 cups water

2 chamomile tea bags

1 tablespoon fresh or dried marigold, parsley, or catnip

1 tablespoon lemon juice (optional; lemon juice lightens, but it can also dry your hair—those with fragile locks are better off without it)

If you have dark hair, you will need:

2 cups water

2 orange pekoe or black tea bags

1 tablespoon fresh or dried sage, rosemary, parsley, or catnip

1 tablespoon beet juice (optional)

continued on next page

If you have red hair, you will need:

1 cup water

1 red hibiscus or rose hips tea bag

1 tablespoon fresh or dried parsley or catnip

$\frac{1}{2}$ cup beet juice (optional)

$\frac{1}{2}$ cup carrot juice, strained (optional)

[1] In a saucepan, bring water to a boil. Remove from heat and add tea bags and herbs. Steep for 15 minutes.

[2] Remove tea bags and strain out the herbs. Allow the infusion to cool to room temperature.

[3] Add the juice, if using.

[4] To use, pour the brew over your hair *after* you condition. It's also a good idea to pour with your head over a bowl, so you can catch the runoff and rinse your hair with it several times. Leave on for a few minutes, then rinse with water. Keep brew away from clothing and the good towels—it will stain fabrics.

Makes one treatment.

Note

You can use the light and red hair infusions as leave-in treatments. Pour the mixture into a spray bottle and mist your hair, then sit in the sun for a while to bring out the highlights.

butterfly
fields

Host a horde of butterfly clips in your twisty tresses for a springy look that's perfect for all-out dance parties, weekend excursions, and Sundays in the park.

You will need:

6 to 8 rubber bands or big clips

Hair spray

6 to 8 butterfly clips

[1] Separate hair into six to eight rows, running from the front of your head to the back, and secure each with a rubberband or clip.

[2] Unclip a section and spray it with hair spray. Starting at the base, twist and twist until you can't twist no more. Secure the tail with a butterfly clip. Continue with the rest of the rows. It doesn't matter if the butterflies don't line up—they're butterflies, not soldiers.

[3] Give the overall scene a shot of hair spray for hold.

medusa
twists

Be a dread-head for a day with these temporary twists.
Pair them with platforms, add lots of beads, and throw on
some funky denim for a one-world Rasta look.

You will need:

Shaving cream (use a product for women,
unless you want to smell like your dad)

Hair spray

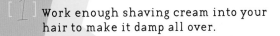

[1] Work enough shaving cream into your
hair to make it damp all over.

2 Separate hair into dreadlock-size
sections. Spray each section with hair
spray and twist, twist, twist, rubbing
between your palms, until you get a dread
effect. Use more hair spray as necessary.

continued on next page

[3] Wear your dreads down or, if you have long hair, tie them back with a kerchief or bundle them together with bright-colored rubber bands. You could also decorate individual dreads by wrapping them in embroidery thread or fabric scraps.

[4] When it's time to de-dreadify, simply wash them out with lots of shampoo, rinse, and then condition.

up~do

When *la dolce vita* calls, you need a high-glamour hair-style to go with that little black dress. Grab your shades and hail a taxi for uptown, because this is it.

You will need:

Ponytail elastic

Approximately 20 hairpins

Hair spray

Big rhinestone brooch

[1] Make a ponytail high on your head. Wrap the tail around a few times to make a chignon (bun). Secure with some of the hairpins. If you have really long hair, you can braid your ponytail first.

[2] Spray liberally with hair spray.

continued on next page

[3] Secure rhinestone brooch to the front of your chignon with hairpins.

[4] Pull on some opera-length gloves, add a string of pearls, and you're ready for Fifth Avenue.

Short Hair Variation

Hair spray and back-comb your hair until you get some volume and height. Smooth it back and slip on a plain black or rhinestone head-band. Voilà! Instant Audrey Hepburn.

"i dream of jeannie"
ponytail

Want a fun new look? Your wish is our command. This sassy ponytail can go sporty or high drama, as you please.

You will need:

Ponytail elastic

Bobby pin

Long hair (still six months away? see note below)

[1] Make a ponytail high on your head. Take a small section of hair from your ponytail and braid it.

[2] Wrap your braid around the base of the ponytail. Secure the end of the braid with a bobby pin.

[3] Fold your arms and blink—your beauty wish has been granted!

Note Is your hair almost long enough, but not quite? Instead of the braid, fix up your ponytail by wrapping a small silk scarf or silk ribbon around the base.

part 5

spa-day ideas

battery charge

Feel like you're running on empty? You need a day of spa-style pampering. Clear your calendar, take the phone off the hook, and indulge in some restful, restorative beauty treatments. On the other hand, maybe your life is practically stress free and you feel downright perky with good health—that's no reason to deny yourself a spa day. Maybe you can get even more relaxed! For the ultimate spa-o-rama described here, you will need to make a few preparations and probably a trip to the drugstore for supplies.

Begin your Battery Charge Spa Day by sleeping late—really late. Try going for a record. See if you can convince a benevolent family member to bring you breakfast in bed (oatmeal with fruit and herbal tea is a good spa-day starter). When you're finally ready to rise, trot off to draw yourself a relaxing Flower Bath (p.96). Surround the tub with candles and bring some trashy magazines to *peruse while you soak. You could also indulge in more bath-time treatments. Slather your hair with Deeply Decadent Conditioner (p. 81) and polish your skin with Vanilla Body Scrub (p. 54). When your fingers and toes have reached maximum prunage, drag yourself out of the tub and dry off. Put your most relaxing music on and give your hands a Butterfingers Hand Treatment (p. 68), and do your feet while you're at it. Follow with a manicure and pedicure. Sip a cup of chamomile or mint tea while your nails dry. Then it's time for lunch and a well deserved nap.*

Note. Spa day is even more fun with a friend (or Mom).

continued on next page

Flower Bath

Why didn't we think of this before?! Picture a rose in full bloom, how delicious it is to breathe in the fragrance, how silky-smooth its petals feel against your cheek. Now imagine feeling that sensation from head to toe. When Aphrodite says she's in the bath, this is what she's talking about.

You will need:

$^1/_2$ cup fresh rose petals

1 tablespoon lavender

2 teaspoons vitamin E oil or liquid glycerin (available at most drugstores)

A splash of rose water or a few drops of lavender or rose essential oil (optional; see page 23 for how to make rose water)

[1] Draw a nice, warm bath. As it's running, add rose petals, lavender, vitamin E oil, and rose water.

[2] Sink in, soak up the heavenly essence of a rose garden in summer, and enjoy.

Makes enough for one bath.

hollywood

glamour day

When Hollywood's glitterati start to feel a little tarnished, they head for the spa and stay there until that golden glow is back to its usual sparkle. A superstar like yourself deserves nothing less. These spa treatments will restore the luster to your tired image. You don't want to disappoint your public.

Start with a bubble bath. Then give yourself an indulgent Hungarian Facial (see facing page). Mix up a Mocktail to sip while you spa (p. 101). For the full spa effect, proceed with a Butterfingers Hand Treatment (p. 68) for your hands and feet, then follow with a manicure and pedicure with fire-engine-red nail polish. Pop in your favorite old movie (at a loss? Roman Holiday, Some Like It Hot, Breakfast at Tiffany's, The Maltese Falcon, or Gentlemen Prefer Blondes should do the trick) to watch while your nails dry. You're ready for your close-up.

Hungarian Facial

This treatment will make you feel just like Zsa Zsa, dahling. It's soooo vahnderful!

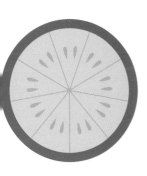

You will need:

Bath towel

Washcloth

Facial cleanser (store-bought, or use the "Breakfast" scrub on p. 31)

2 cups water

2 herbal tea bags

Mask (store-bought, or use your own Instant Milk-and-Honey Mask on p. 24 or the Greek Goddess Mask on p. 26)

2 cucumber slices

Toner (store-bought, or use the Apple-a-Day Toner on p. 18 or the Tingly Toner on p. 20)

Moisturizer (store-bought, or use the Desert Rose Moisturizer on p. 22 or the Emerald Emollient on p. 28)

continued on next page

1 Put your hair in a towel turban. Soak the washcloth with warm (not hot) water. Lie down, place the washcloth on your face, and keep it there for a few minutes.

2 Wash your face with your cleanser.

3 Following the directions for "Dinner" on p. 33, give yourself a steam treatment. Rinse your face with cool water and pat dry.

4 Apply your mask, avoiding the eye area. Leave on for 15 minutes or as long as directed, if you are using one from the store. Place cucumber slices over your eyes while you bask in the mask. (It's nice to have a soothing CD spinning while you luxuriate.) Rinse your face thoroughly.

5 Apply toner and follow with moisturizer. Admire your healthy, glowing skin. You ought to be in pictures.

Makes one treatment.

100

Mocktail

On spa day you want something a little fancier than fruit punch. Try this sophisticated sparkler instead.

You will need:

Tumbler

Ice cubes

$\frac{1}{4}$ cup cranberry juice

Measuring cup

$1\frac{1}{2}$ teaspoons lime juice (fresh or bottled, plain or sweetened as desired)

Club soda or lemon-lime soda

Twist of lime (a thin strip of lime rind)

continued on next page

[1] Fill tumbler three-quarters full with ice. Pour cranberry juice into measuring cup, add lime juice, stir, and pour the mixture over the ice. Add soda to the top of the glass.

[2] Garnish with twist of lime.

[3] Enjoy. Here's looking at you, kid.

Makes one drink.

aromatherapy
spa day

Maybe you've noticed how certain smells affect your mood. If you happen to have strolled through a grove of eucalyptus trees lately (who hasn't?), you probably felt your mind clear, your spirit lift, and your lips form a tranquil smile. And what about the smell of freshly baked bread—have you ever been in a bad mood in a bakery?

The principle is called "aromatherapy" and with a supply of five to ten basic essential oils from health food stores and bath shops, you can practice it at home. The basics can include peppermint, lavender, eucalyptus, rose, jasmine, almond, various citrus flavors, and any number of other delicious smells. You might start with peppermint and lavender and then add to your collection from there. Whatever you choose, always store essential oils in glass, not plastic.

Start your Aromatherapy Spa Day with an Aromatherapy Bath (see recipe, p. 104). Then massage your feet, hands, calves, or temples with Aromatherapy Massage Oil (p. 106). Finally, make up some Scent Saucers (p. 108) to sniff. Take a deep breath: good air in, bad air out.

continued on next page

Aromatherapy Bath

Shouldn't a bath do more than get you clean? This one gives you a new attitude.

For courage and stamina, you will need:

4 drops marjoram essential oil

4 drops ylang-ylang essential oil

3 drops jasmine essential oil

For calming relaxation, you will need:

4 drops cypress essential oil

2 drops cedarwood essential oil

2 drops sandalwood essential oil

For clarity and energy (especially when you have a cold), you will need:

5 drops eucalyptus essential oil

5 drops peppermint essential oil

4 drops lavender essential oil

[1] Draw a nice warm bath. Add the appropriate combination of essential oil drops and swoosh around to mix.

[2] Get in, breathe deeply, and soak up the good vibes.

Makes enough for one bath.

Note If your bath is an evening ritual, light a candle or two and turn down the lights. Natural paraffin or beeswax candles give off a relaxing, golden glow. Be sure to use unscented candles in order to preserve the delicate aromas you've created.

Aromatherapy Massage Oils

Rub away tension and soreness with these easy blends. You can massage your own feet, calves, hands, and temples.

For treating sore muscles (great for the day after an extreme workout), you will need:

$1/4$ cup sweet almond oil

3 drops birch essential oil

3 drops chamomile essential oil

3 drops ginger essential oil

3 drops lavender essential oil

3 drops rosemary essential oil

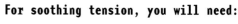

For soothing tension, you will need:

$1/4$ cup sweet almond oil

3 drops lavender essential oil

2 drops chamomile essential oil

1 drop vetiver (smells like grass) essential oil

[1] Pour almond oil into a small glass bowl (or a glass measuring cup).

[2] Add the appropriate essential oil drops and stir until combined.

[3] Give yourself a foot, hand, or calf massage using the oil mixture. If you're using the tension massage oil, help yourself relax by gently rubbing it into your temples, too.

Makes one treatment.

Note

This mixture will keep, so you may want to double the recipe and pour it into a glass bottle with a lid. An aromatherapy massage also makes a great gift for friends and family. If you are feeling generous, grab the lucky recipient and soak their feet for five minutes in a tub of warm water with a spoonful of baking soda in it. Lift one foot and massage with the oil. Then do the other foot. The same routine works wonders on hands.

Scent Saucers

In the mood for a wonderful indulgence? Got a nasty case of the blues? Mix up little dishes of magically mood-altering scent. Retire to the nearest hippie den (or your bedroom) and chill.

You will need:

Boiling water

Ceramic cup and saucer

Essential oils (choose one of the following aromatherapy combinations)

Herbal tea bag (optional; use chamomile for peace or banishing the blues, or mint for boosting creativity and energy)

To inspire creativity:
2 drops peppermint essential oil
2 drops rosemary essential oil
2 drops orange essential oil

To restore pep and vigor:
2 drops peppermint essential oil
2 drops rosemary essential oil
2 drops lavender essential oil

To fend off the blues:
2 drops bergamot essential oil
2 drops geranium essential oil
2 drops melissa essential oil
2 drops orange essential oil

For peace and serenity:
10 drops lavender essential oil
5 drops chamomile essential oil

continued on next page

[1] Put water on to boil in a teakettle or saucepan. Combine the appropriate essential oil drops in the saucer.

[2] When the water boils, fill the cup with water. Add a tea bag if you want a cup of tea after your aromatherapy. Place the cup on your nightstand or anywhere near where you plan to relax. Set the saucer, with the oils in it, on top of the cup. The heat of the water will help release the fragrance of the oils.

[3] Lie down and close your eyes. Breathe in deeply and out slowly and completely. In deeply, out slowly and completely. Smell your way to a wonderful day. When you are thoroughly relaxed and refreshed, drink your tea or a tall glass of water.

Makes one treatment.

half-hour

mini~spa

Places to go, people to see, and only half an hour of you-time. Make the most of it with these speedy treats for any time of day.

Mix up a Five-Minute Mask (p. 112). While you've got your mask on, you can give yourself a Flying Fingers Hand Treatment (p. 114). Then wash up, paint your nails with fast-drying nail polish, and douse yourself with Speedy Spritzer (p. 115). Zero to gorgeous in half an hour flat.

continued on next page

Five-Minute Mask

Get fresh-faced fast with this quick skin brightener that mixes up quickly and works wonders in a flash. For oily skin, egg white tones while astringent grapefruit juice banishes oil and tightens pores. For dry skin, banana and honey soothe, moisturize, and leave your cheeks baby smooth.

If you have oily skin, you will need:

1 egg white (see note on page 27)

2 teaspoons grapefruit juice

If you have dry skin, you will need:

½ banana, thoroughly mashed

1 teaspoon honey

[1] In a bowl, stir or whisk your mask ingredients together until blended. Apply mask to face, avoiding the eye area.

[2] Leave mask on for five minutes, then rinse well.

Makes one mask.

Flying Fingers Hand Treatment

Your hands get a workout every day. Make it up to them with a few minutes of intense moisturizing action. Smooth out rough hands, in the time it takes to snap your fingers, with this speedy answer to soap, dirt, calluses, and all the other assaults on silky fingers.

You will need:

1 tablespoon oil (olive oil is best, but any oil will do)

2 small plastic bags

Hand towel

Hand lotion

[1] Microwave oil in a small dish for a few seconds. You want it just slightly warm, not hot.

[2] Rub oil on your hands. Put hands in plastic bags, then tuck them into a hand towel. Veg out for five minutes.

[3] Rinse off oil with warm water. Pat hands dry and rub with hand lotion. Now don't those paws feel baby-soft?

Makes one treatment.

Speedy Spritzer

Back when bathing was considered a vice, a bit of perfume and a splash of water was the closest anyone came to taking the plunge. Times have changed, but there may still be those days when you need to dash without having a thorough wash. When that's the case, freshen up the old French way with this easy spritzer.

You will need:

1 cup water

5 to 7 drops of your favorite perfume oil

Spray bottle

[1] Pour water and perfume oil into spray bottle and shake well.

[2] Spritz your hair, your face, even your clothes. You'll get a nice, long bath someday, but for now, you look and smell like you just stepped out of one, you sneaky devil.

Makes 8 ounces.

the seven steps

Take these seven steps to put your best face forward.

[1]
Wash

Before you create the masterpiece, you must prime the canvas. Get off all the grease and grime by washing your face gently but thoroughly with warm water and mild soap or facial cleanser. Pat dry.

[2]
Mask

Now that you're a clean teen, get grubby again. Glop on a tingling, tightening mask. Dry skin? Mix up an Instant Milk-and-Honey Mask (p. 24). Oily? Make yourself a Greek Goddess Mask (p. 26).

[3]
Rinse

Rinse off the mask goo with warm water. Gently pat face dry. Never rub. You're not buffing a car.

[4] Steam

After you've given your
face a workout, it's time to
give it a sauna. Open your pores
with a steam treatment (Three
Square Meals for Your Face,
"Dinner", p. 33) and say "so
long" to impurities.

[5] Refresh

Close your pores
with a quick rinse in
cool water. Pat dry.
Ahhhhh.

[6] Tone

Put some color in your
cheeks with a splash of
rejuvenating toner. Dry
skin? Use Apple-A-Day Toner
(p. 18). Oily? Use Tingly
Toner (p. 20).

[7] Moisturize

Seal in the goodness
with a drop or two of
soothing moisture. Dry skin?
Use rich, creamy Emerald
Emollient (p. 28). Oily? Try
light, quenching Desert
Rose Moisturizer (p. 22).

Seven steps later you're primed,
purified, and polished.

Step eight: go sparkle!

decorative

labels

Photocopy these pages onto sticker paper. Cut out your
labels, peel off the backings, and label away!

tingly toner

created by_____

desert rose
moisturizer

created by_____

a bit of the
bubbly

created by_____

emerald
emollient

created by_____

make a splash

created by_____

cocoa cream

created by_____

country~fresh
milk bath

created by_____

peppermint
toe~tingler

created by_____

glitter
glow

apple~a~day toner

created by_____

shine
on

created by_____

created by_____

created by_____

created by_____

created by_____

created by_____

119

the end